11/00
4
12/04

Rookie
Read-About® Health

W9-CPF-932

Smelling

By Sharon Gordon

Consultants
Nanci R. Vargus, Ed.D.
Primary Multiage Teacher
Decatur Township Schools, Indianapolis, Indiana

Jan Jenner, Ph.D.

Children's Press®
A Division of Scholastic Inc.
New York   Toronto   London   Auckland   Sydney
Mexico City   New Delhi   Hong Kong
Danbury, Connecticut

Designer: Herman Adler Design
Photo Researcher: Caroline Anderson
The photo on the cover shows a boy smelling a flower.

Library of Congress Cataloging-in-Publication Data

Gordon, Sharon.
    Smelling / by Sharon Gordon.
      p. cm. — (Rookie read-about health)
    Includes index.
    Summary: A simple introduction to the sense of smell.
    ISBN 0-516-22292-9 (lib. bdg.)   0-516-25991-1 (pbk.)
    1. Smell—Juvenile literature. [1. Smell. 2. Senses and sensation.]
  I. Title. II. Series.
  QP458 .G67   2001
  612.8'6—dc21

                             00-060125

Something smells delicious!

4

The hot apple pie is almost ready. But how will everyone know where to find it?

Their sense of smell will tell them where to go!

Smelling is one of the five senses. The others are seeing, hearing, tasting and touching.

8

The sense of smell
begins with your nose.

All kinds of smells
are floating in the air
around you.

When you take a breath
of air, you take in lots
of smells.

The air carrying the smells goes into your nose.

It moves deep inside your head and into your nasal cavity (NAY-zuhl KAV-i-tee).

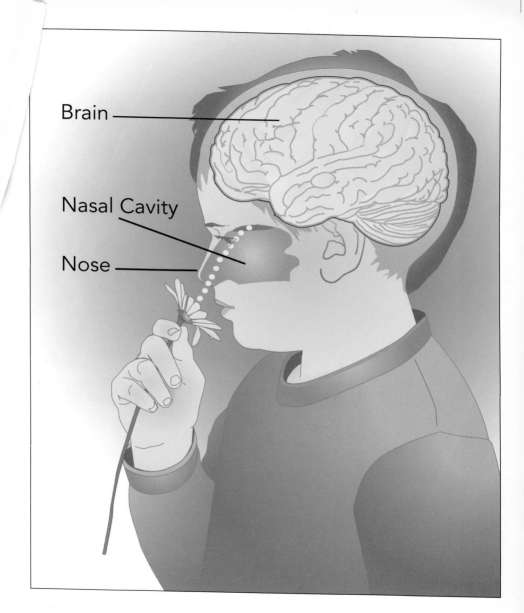

Brain

Nasal Cavity

Nose

12

There are millions of tiny little hairs inside your nasal cavity.

These special hairs "catch" the floating smells.

These hairs tell your brain
what the smells are.

That is how you smell things.

Do you love to wake up
to the smell of breakfast
cooking?

Add some cinnamon to the pancake batter. Can you smell the difference?

Walk through a flower garden. Can you smell the difference between a rose and a lilac? No peeking!

Rose

Lilac

Do you like the smell
of perfume?

There are so many kinds
to choose from!

21

22

Not all smells are good.

A scared skunk gives off
a very bad smell.

Watch out—don't let
him spray you! Or you
will smell bad, too.

Food that is rotten smells bad. The smell lets you know not to eat it.

The smell of smoke warns you of danger.

Is there a fire nearby?

Some smells can even make you cry!

Onions

Words You Know

garden

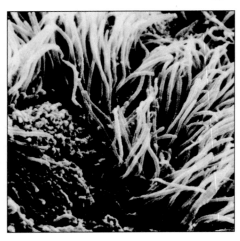

hairs

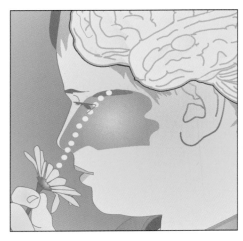

nasal cavity

30

nose

perfume

skunk

smoke

31

Index

About the Author

Sharon Gordon is a writer living in Midland Park, New Jersey. She and her husband have three school-aged children and a spoiled pooch. Together they enjoy visiting the Outer Banks of North Carolina as often as possible.

Photo Credits

Photographs ©: Corbis-Bettmann/Jerry Cooke: 29; Nance S. Trueworthy: 3; Peter Arnold Inc./Jeff Greenberg: cover; Photo Researchers, NY: 19 bottom (Alan L. Detrick), 22, 31 bottom left (Jeff Lepore); PhotoEdit: 15 (Rachel Epstein), 25 (Novastock), 18, 26, 30 top, 31 bottom right, (D. Young-Wolff); Rigoberto Quinteros: 21, 31 top right; Stock Boston: 14 (Dean Abramson), 16 (Mike & Carol Werner); Superstock, Inc.: 7, 8, 19 top, 31 top left; The Stock Market: 17 (Chuck Savage); The Stock Market: 4 (Eleanor Thompson); Visuals Unlimited/Veronika Burmeister: 12, 30 bottom left.

Illustration by Patricia Rasch.